Looking at our Environment

Seána Miller

You can look up the meaning of the words in **bold type** in the glossary at the back of the book.

Acknowledgements

The map on page 15, based on the Ordnance Survey Maps with permission of HMSO, is reproduced by permission of Geographers' A–Z Map Co. Ltd, and is © Crown Copyright. The map on page 11 is based on OS mapping with HMSO permission, © Crown Copyright.

The publishers would like to thank the following for permission to reproduce photographs:
Ace Photo Agency (4A); Aerofilms (14A); J Allan Cash Ltd (13D, 17B, 21B, 23C, 30A, 32A, 35B, 36A, 40A, 44A); Aspect Picture Library (10A, 17A, 21A); Heather Angel/Biofotos (29C, 45D); Robert Harding Picture Library (28A, 34A); Hutchison Library (13A, 23A, 24B, 33A, 41B, 43B); Impact Photos/Paul Forster (37B); Impact Photos/Alain le Garsmeur (43A); Frank Lane Picture Agency (45C); Panos Pictures (13B, 33A); Picturepoint Ltd (6A, B, C, 13C, 14A, 18A, 23B, 32B, 39A, 44B, 45D);

The publishers have made every effort to trace copyright holders. However, if any material has been incorrectly acknowledged, we would be pleased to correct this at the earliest opportunity.

© Seána Miller. First published 1993
Designed by Miller, Craig & Cocking
Illustrated by Nick Hawken
Printed in Spain by Mateu Cromo Artes Graficas SA.

93 94 95 96 97 10 9 8 7 6 5 4 3 2 1

Heinemann Educational
A Division of Heinemann Publishers (Oxford) Ltd
Halley Court, Jordan Hill, Oxford OX2 8EJ.

OXFORD LONDON EDINBURGH
MADRID ATHENS BOLOGNA PARIS
MELBOURNE SYDNEY AUCKLAND SINGAPORE TOKYO
IBADAN NAIROBI HARARE GABORONE
PORTSMOUTH NH (USA)

Contents

HOW Looking at our Environment

Page

The human environment

1	Where on earth do you live?	4
2	Settlements, the place to live!	6
3	Is your map mental?	8
4	A new view?	10
5	Map matters	12
6	Planning a change?	14
7	Busy places, quiet places	16

The physical environment

8	What about the weather?	18
9	Where does the rain go?	20
10	Soil – more than mud pies!	22
11	From rain to rivers?	24
12	Looking at valleys	26
13	How a river floods and feeds	28
14	World weather	30
15	Soil on the move	32
16	Where's the nearest volcano?	34
17	Volcanoes – not just hot-headed mountains!	36
18	When the earth moves	38

The effects of human activity

19	A world full of resources?	40
20	The ancient forests vs the beefburger	42
21	Looking after our environment	44
	Glossary	46

1 Where on earth do you live?

It's important to know where you live. It's not just a matter of saying your address and making sure you don't get lost on the way back from your neighbour's house! Knowing where you live in relation to your school, your community, your country and the rest of the world, will help you to understand why people live and work in certain places.

Photo A Keeping out the cold

Sometimes people change the way they live to suit the physical environment. For example, people who live in very cold places usually build houses with lots of insulation to keep them warm inside.

More often, people change the **landscape** so much by building towns and cities, roads and railways, that we call it the 'human environment'.

Looking at our Environment

A good way to start finding out about the environment in which you live is to use different types of maps. Look at these maps.

The world

The United Kingdom

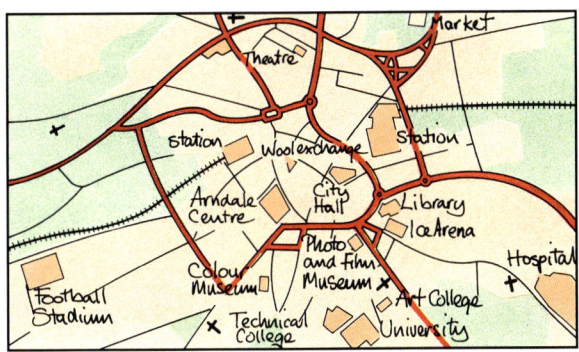

A city

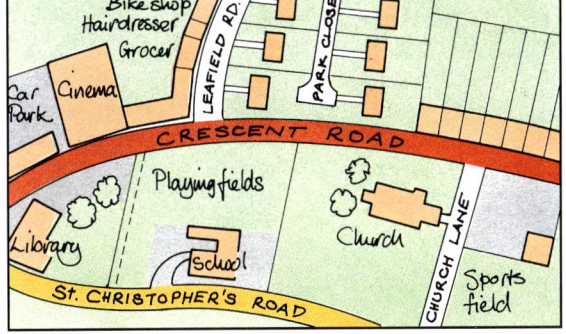

A street

Things to do

1. What types of map are shown? What is the main difference between them?
2. Use an atlas to find out where you live. Make a list of all the maps you can find in the atlas which show the place where you live.
3. Use the co-ordinates grid on Activity Sheet 1 to locate the region of the British Isles where you live. What are the co-ordinates?
4. Make a list of three other places on the map you can identify. What are their co-ordinates?

2 Settlements, the place to live!

Think about the **settlement** where you live. Is it a town, a village or a city?

A village Photo A

Photo B A town

Photo C A city

Whatever the size, most settlements have features in common like roads, houses and shops. In order to identify one place from another, all settlements have names. Within a settlement the streets and roads are also named, otherwise, how would your friends be able to send you a postcard when they go on holiday?

Looking at our Environment

Sometimes the names of settlements (and their streets) will give you a clue as to how old the place is or why it was built there. Remember that even the biggest cities were once small settlements.

Picture A Who will receive the postcard from Sam?

Things to do

1. Find out which of your local street/road names give clues about why the place was built there. Do any names give clues about when the street was built?
2. How are the roads and buildings arranged in your settlement? Draw a picture plan and use labels to show what it is like.
3. Think of a physical feature in the settlement where you live. Can you name it? Has this feature anything to do with why the settlement started there? (Remember that if you live in a city or town you may have to look very carefully to find the physical features because they might be hidden in and around the buildings and streets.)

3 Is your map mental?

It is important for you to look around and think about the environment where you live. Using a large-scale map of the school area, you can probably work out what the buildings are around the school, and how they are placed in your settlement. But what if you didn't have the map to help you? Would you remember what and where the buildings and the roads are?

From home to school

When you have a picture in your head of an area that you know or of a route you often take, this is called a **mental map**. You may not be able to remember all the things that are there but you should be able to think of the main features.

Looking at our Environment

Things to do

1. On a big sheet of paper, make a chart like this for the buildings in your area.

Buildings	Co-ordinates	Places to live	Places to work	Places to play

   Use a large-scale map of your locality to jog your memory. Fill in the chart to:

   a) show the kinds of buildings they are by ticking the right column, and

   b) give four figure co-ordinates to locate them.

2. Pick out two of the places on the map that you have mentioned on your chart. Using a ruler, can you measure how far apart they are 'as the crow flies' (the shortest distance between two places)? Use the scale at the bottom of the map to work out the real distance in kilometres.

3. Draw your own mental map of a route you know well: for example, from home to school or to the local shop.

   Think about how the buildings and other features are shown on the large scale map when you draw yours. Don't forget that you can add labels too.

4 A new view?

When you study other places you will not usually have the benefit of your own mental map of the area. Look at this photo of Durham.

Photo A Looking down on Durham

How do you think the photo was taken? What mental map of Durham does the photo give you?

Looking at our Environment

Here is an **Ordnance Survey map** of Durham. How does it help you form a mental map? What details does the map give you that the photo doesn't?

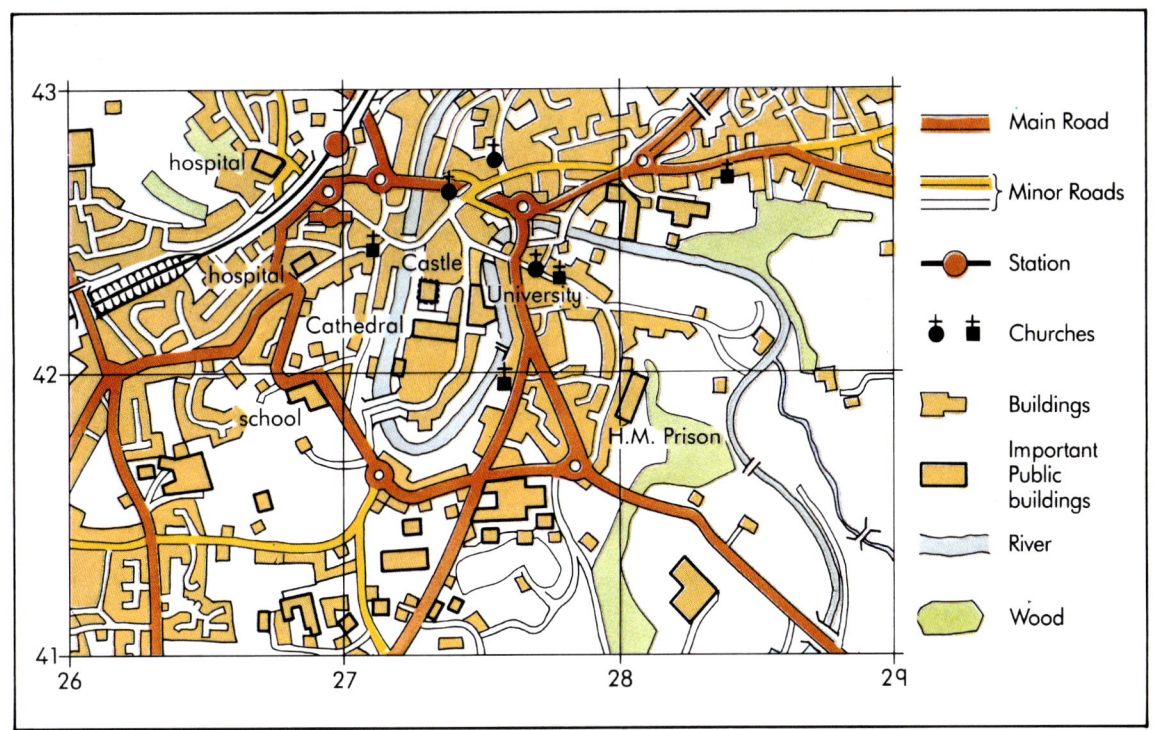

Ordnance Survey map of Durham

Things to do

1. Look at Photo A and the Ordnance Survey map of Durham. Can you find the castle? What is its grid reference?
2. Using Photo A, name at least two features which give a clue why a town grew up here. Say whether they are 'physical' or 'human' features. You can use the Ordnance Survey map as well to help you.
3. Draw a sketch map of part of the area shown on the photo/map which includes the river. You can make up **symbols** to represent buildings and other features. Remember to use a key to show what they are!

11

5 Map matters

You can use atlases and globes to find out where to locate different places in the world. A globe shows you the whole of planet Earth. Because of this, the **scale** is very small.

In an atlas, however, you see different parts of the world and at different scales.

CONTENTS LIST
- 2-3   Scale and Direction
- 4-5   Latitude and Longitude
- 6-7   Graphs, Diagrams and Charts
- 8-9   England and Wales
- 10   Scotland
- 11   Ireland
- 12   British Isles: Relief of Land
- 13   British Isles: Geology and Water Supply
- 14   British Isles: Climate and Weather
- 15   British Isles: Counties and Regions
- 16-17 British Isles: People
- 18   British Isles: Food Supply
- 19   British Isles: Power Supply
- 20   British Isles: Trade and Industry
- 21   British Isles: Travel and Leisure
- 22   Europe: Relief of Land
- 23   Europe: Countries
- 24-25 European Themes
- 26-27 Western Europe
- 28-29 Central Europe
- 30-31 Southern Europe
- 32   Scandinavia
- 33   Asia
- 34-35 South Asia
- 36   North America
- 37   South America
- 38   Pacific Ocean
- 39   Australia and New Ze[aland]
- 40   Africa

Picture A Using the Contents Page

Picture B Find the country. Find the town.

Use an atlas to find where you live and the city of Durham.

Looking at our Environment

People live in all these places.

Photo A Oasis settlement in Sahara desert

Photo B Dhaka

Photo C Shanghai

Photo D Washington DC

Things to do

1. Find a map in the atlas which has a similar scale to the one on the globe. Can you find the settlement where you live? Would it be better to use a different map? Use the index to find another map that will clearly show your home town.
2. Mark where you live on the map on Activity Sheet 7. Also mark Durham on the map and name the places marked A–D. What do you notice about where these places are found?
3. Look at the world map on Activity Sheet 8. Matching the locations A–E with the captions at the side will help you to work out why people live in these places.

6 Planning a change?

Within the human environment things are always changing, but at different speeds or rates. The number of people (**population**) changes, the jobs that people do (**employment**) change, the size of towns, villages and cities change.

Because these changes happen all the time in all sorts of places, we have to plan ahead to make sure that there are enough houses, schools and other services for people.

Council approves trading estate

Company's land bid

"Traffic chaos will follow," warns Councillor

National company puts Warrington on the map

Photo A Vertical aerial photo of Warrington

Looking at our Environment

Warrington is in north west England. It is right in the middle of the British Isles. In the past ten years there have been many changes in and around the town. This map shows the same area of Warrington as you can see in the photo.

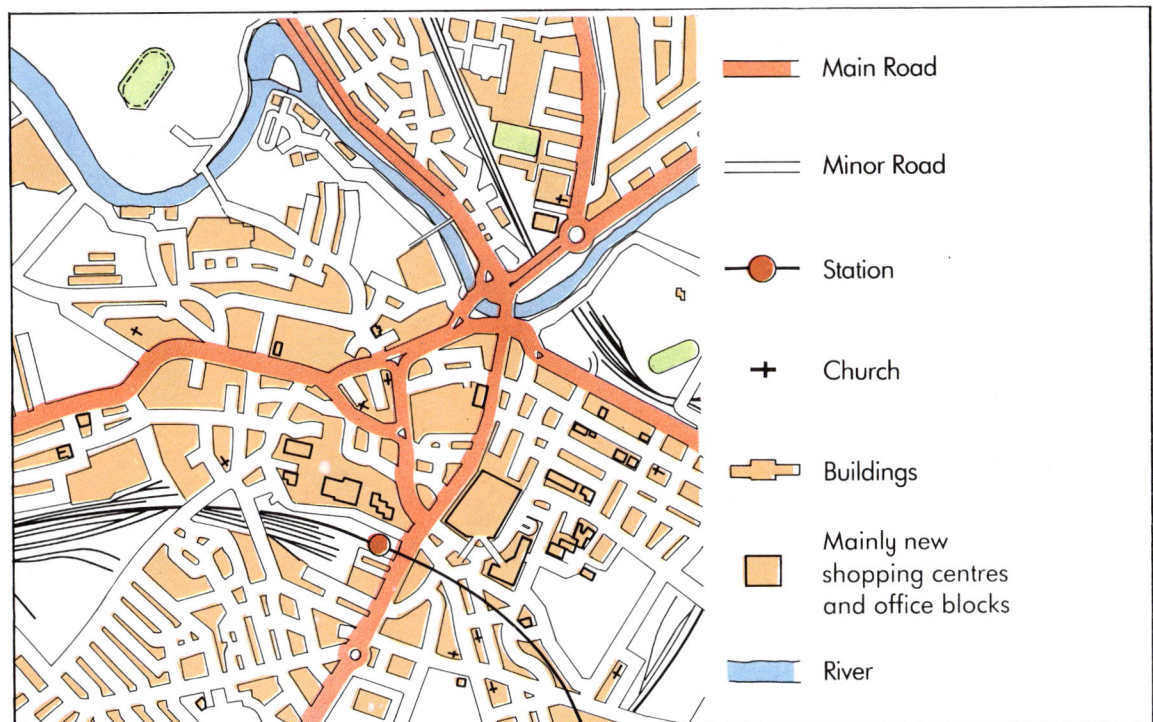

Things to do

1. Write three sentences to describe the layout of the town, using the photo and the map.
2. Look at the newspaper cuttings on page 14 and say what changes you think have taken place. How do you think these changes will affect the people who live and work in the area?
3. Design a brochure to advertise why people should move to Warrington. You could draw a sketch map of part of the town to show the location of places where people could come to live or where they could work.

7 Busy places, quiet places

Why do you think some places are more crowded than others?

The population of the United Kingdom is about 57 million – that's a lot of people!

The map shows a pattern of where people live in the United Kingdom. It's called a population density map. Look in an atlas to find a similar map.

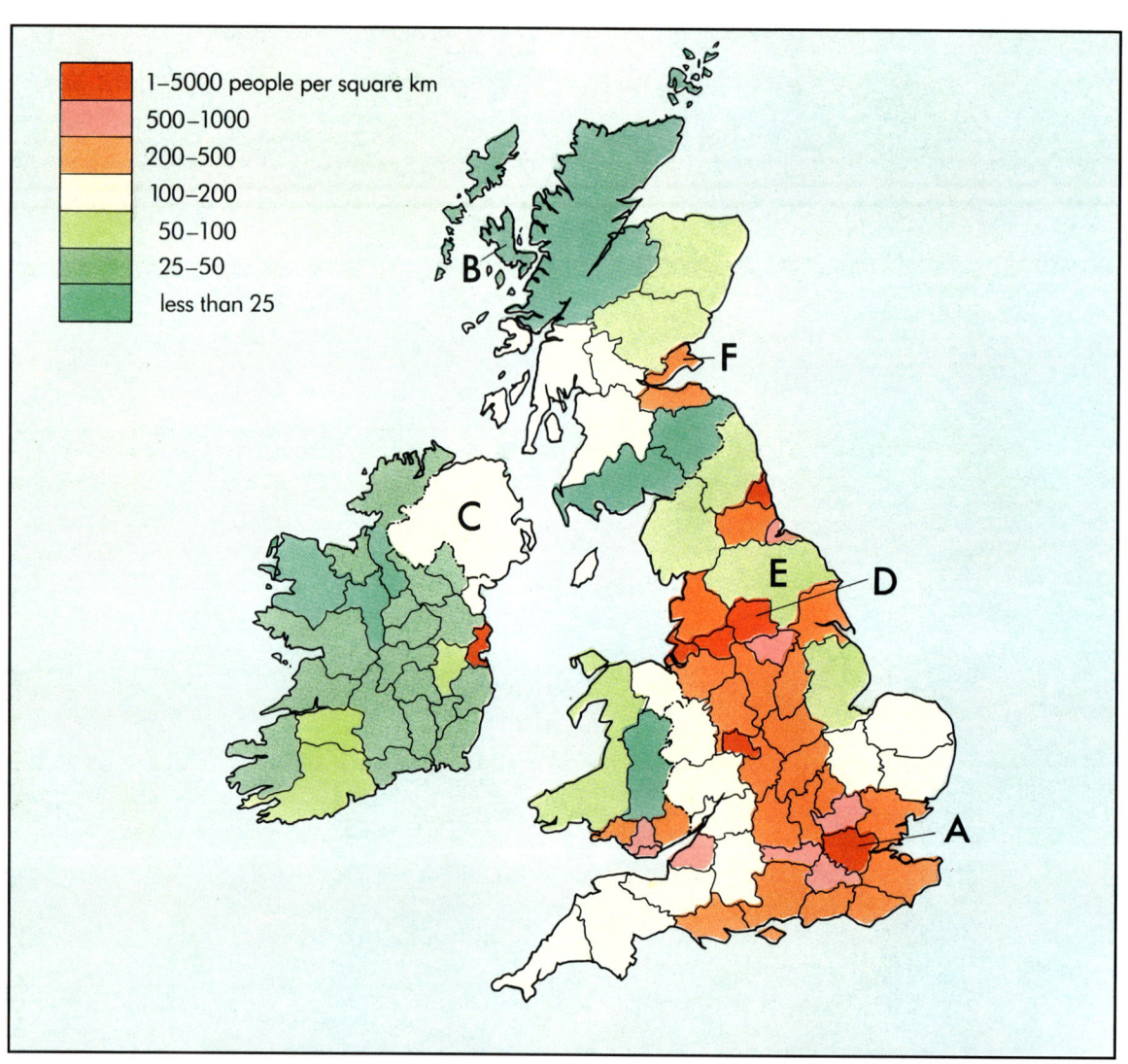

Map A Population density in the UK

The south east region of the country, which includes the capital city of London, is one of the most highly populated areas. Nearly 7 million people live in London.

Looking at our Environment

When a place has many people living there it is said to be **densely populated**. When only a few people live in a place it is **sparsely populated**. Do you live in a place that is sparsely populated or densely populated?

Photo A London

Photo B The Isle of Skye

Things to do

1. Using Map A, say whether the places marked A–F are a) densely populated, b) sparsely populated, or c) in between.
2. Look at an atlas map that shows the physical landscape of the British Isles. Compare this map with the population density map on page 16. How do physical features affect where people live?
3. With a partner, talk about why you think so many people live in towns and cities rather than in the country.
4. A family living in the country is thinking about moving to town. Make a chart to say why it would be good for them to move to live in a busy town. Make a second chart to say why they might not like the change.

8 What about the weather?

Where people choose to live in the world is affected by the weather. It affects what crops can be grown for food and materials. It even affects how long people can work during the day! Can you think why?

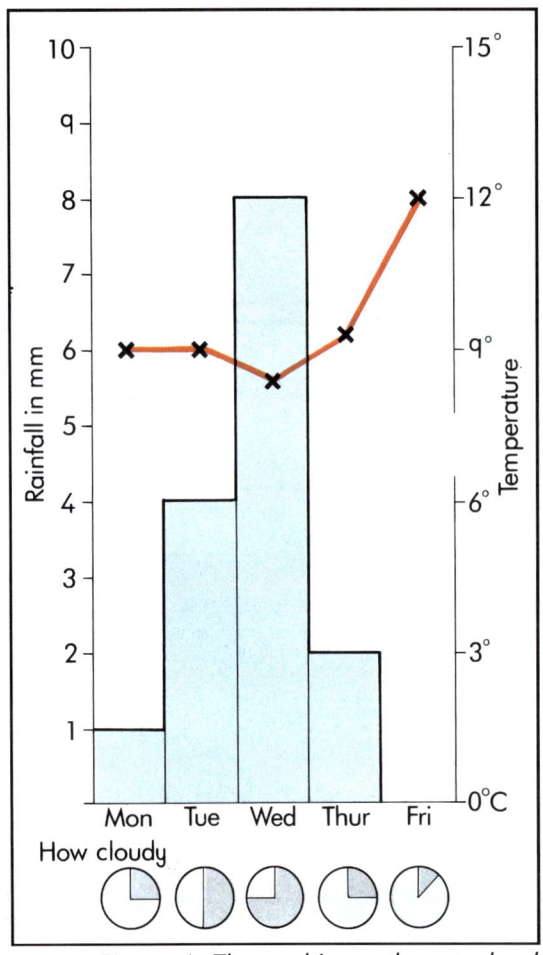

Picture A The week's weather at school

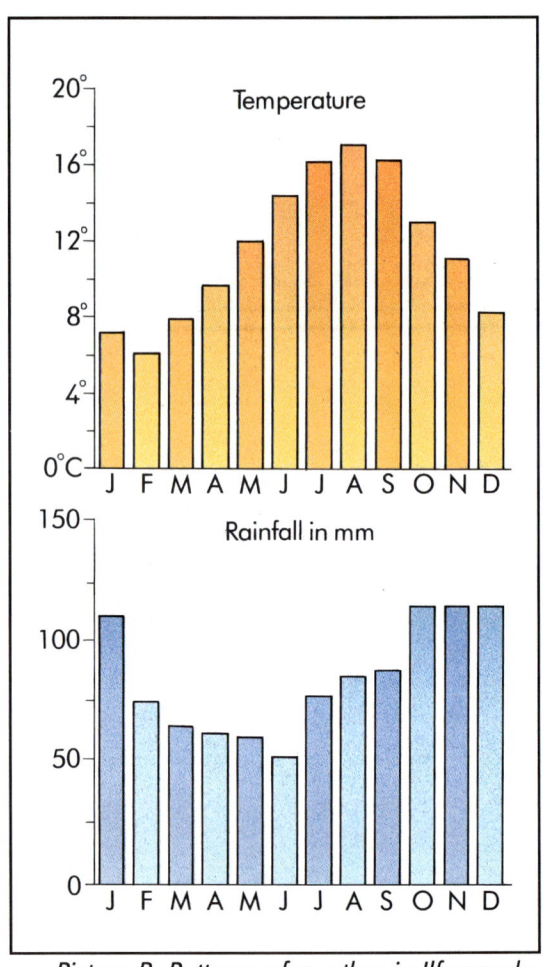

Picture B Patterns of weather in Ilfracombe

On the same day the weather can be very different between one region and another in the British Isles. Sometimes it changes a lot in the same place in one day! Because of this, it is important to measure and record what the weather is like each day. Over a period of time we can use these measurements to work out a pattern of weather. The average of these measurements over a period of time tells us about the climate.

Looking at our Environment

Photo A Will it be sunny tomorrow?

Things to do

1. Measure the weather at school over one week. Draw a map to show how to get to the measuring site that you have chosen. Add labels to show what equipment you have decided to use. Give your map a title.
2. Devise a recording sheet to record your measurements of the temperature, rainfall, clouds and wind. You need to take your measurements every day for a week. How many times a day will you take them?
3. At the end of the week, draw bar charts to show the daily weather. You could choose a different colour for each day of the week.

9 Where does the rain go?

Rain, hail, snow, frost, fog, mist and sleet are all different forms of water which fall to the ground. When water falls in any of these forms it is called precipitation. Usually when you see that it is wet outside, it is because it has been raining. But where does all the water go? Sometimes you can see that the rainwater forms puddles. Other times it seems to disappear very quickly. This is because of the different surfaces that the water lands on.

*Photo A Sand on a beach soaks up water and is **permeable**.*

*Photo B If the water runs off it, a surface is called **impermeable**.*

These different surfaces can be part of the human or the physical environment. The main differences occur underneath the surface. The temperature and the wind will also affect what happens to the rainwater.

Looking at our Environment

Photo C When a permeable surface has so much water on it that no more can sink in, it is called **waterlogged**.

Things to do

1. Keep a diary of your weather measurements. Include in your diary a list of the different surfaces on which the rain falls.
2. Make a chart like this one and fill in the chart from your list:

Water sinks in quickly (permeable)	Water flows over slope (impermeable)	Water forms puddles (waterlogged)

3. Do a detailed drawing to show where the rainwater goes after falling on the roof of your school. Can you show what happens to it once it gets below the surface? Put labels on your drawing.

10 Soil – more than mud pies!

Soil is usually permeable or porous to rainwater. It is like this because it is made up of tiny pieces of crushed rock and bits of dead leaves. This has happened over thousands of years. Look at the drawing below which shows a soil profile.

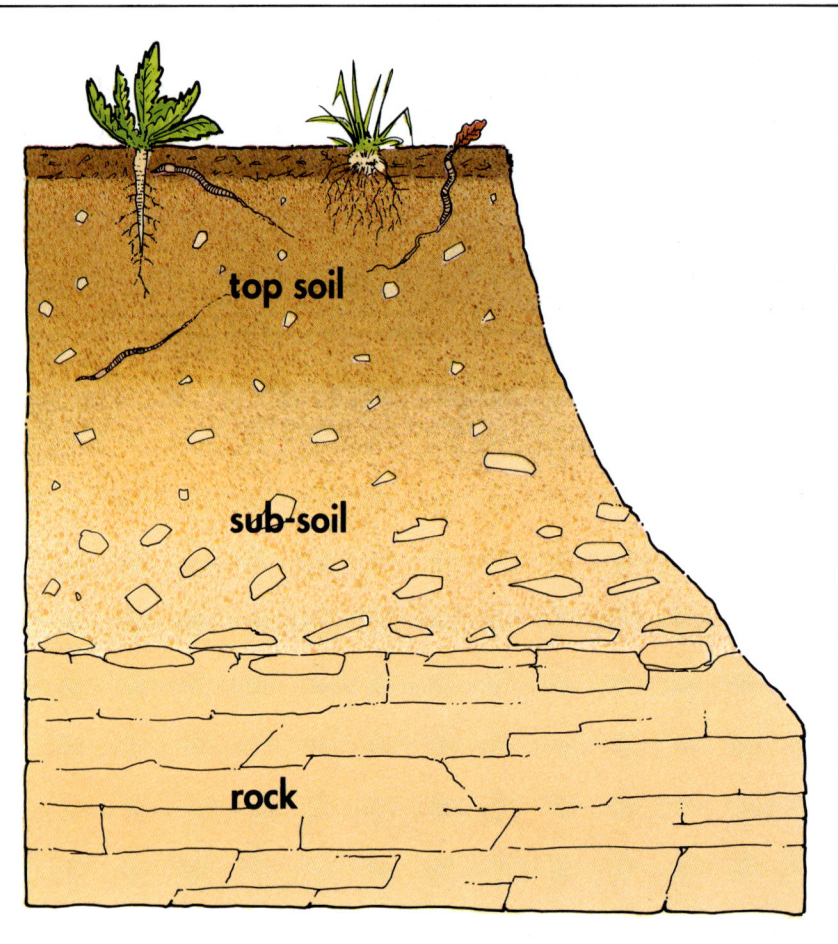

*Dead leaves, twigs and worms help to make the **soil** fertile.*

The soil here is not as good as the top soil, and there are more stones.

*This rocky layer is called **'parent material'** because it is broken down to form the soil.*

Picture A Soil profile

Soil is an important **natural resource**. There are many different types, depending on the climate and the rocks beneath.

The type of soil affects the way that land can be used. If the soil is rich it can be used to grow crops like wheat and barley. If the soil is less good it may be used for grazing animals. Remember, some land will also be used for buildings and roads and some will be left as rough ground.

Looking at our Environment

How the soil is used in any one place depends in part on the position of the site. Is it sunny or shady, windy or sheltered? Is there water nearby to make it cooler? The soil on a north facing hill slope will be different from a south facing one. Can you think which will be warmer? The direction which a place faces is called the **aspect**.

Another factor which can change the soil temperature is the colour! Darker surfaces like soil (or tarmac) become warmer than light surfaces such as grass (or concrete).

Photo A A dark surface

Photo B A light surface

Things to do

1. Measure the temperature of the soil (just below the surface) on the north side of the school building and the south side. Is there a difference? Measure the air temperature as well.
2. Make a chart to show the temperatures for each side. How might the differences affect the soil and what grows there?
3. On a very windy day, do you sometimes take shelter? Make a list of the different places you could take cover.

11 From rain to rivers?

Rivers are really amazing! They begin as little more than a trickle of water high in the mountains, and carve their way through the landscape to finish at the sea. They don't just start anywhere. They must have high rainfall before they can get going, and an impermeable surface like hard rock.

A mountain stream   Photo A

When the rainwater can't sink in, it trickles down the slope. These trickles are called **rills**. A few of these rills join up and form small streams.

It is hard to say just where a river starts. The **source** of the river is the whole area within the **river basin** where it begins to form.

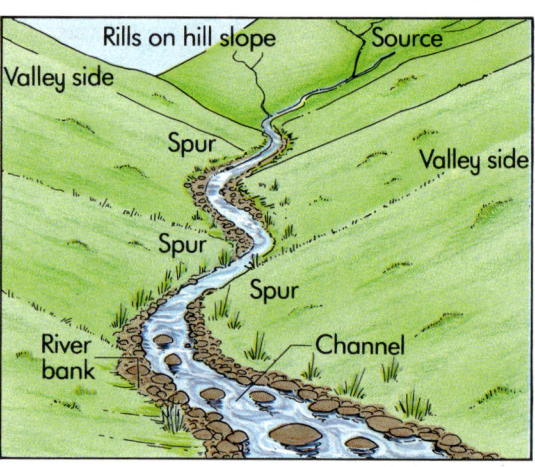

Picture A   The source of a river

As the rills run together down a slope, they follow the shape of the surface. Soon they start to drag along little fragments of rock and soil. These fragments, bouncing and scraping along in the water, begin to damage the rock surface. This is just the start of how rivers change and shape the land on the way to the sea.

Picture B Damage to the river bed

Things to do

1. Talk with your classmates about a hilly place in the British Isles that you know of or that you have seen pictures of. Make a list of as many places as you can think of and find them on a map.
2. Choose one of the places from your list and use a map to see if there is a river nearby. Can you find the river source from the map? What are its four figure co-ordinates?
3. Think about what happens to rainwater that sinks into the ground in high places. Where does it go? What happens to make the water join the river?
4. Draw a flow chart to show what you know so far about how a river starts. You could label it, 'From rain to river'.

12 Looking at valleys

Unless the ground surface is very soft or dry, rainwater on its own doesn't cause much damage. But as small rock fragments and soil are bounced along in the running water, they begin to cut a groove, forming a **channel** and a channel bed. This damage is called **erosion**. Bigger streams can push along heavier bits of rocks and cut the channel deeper.

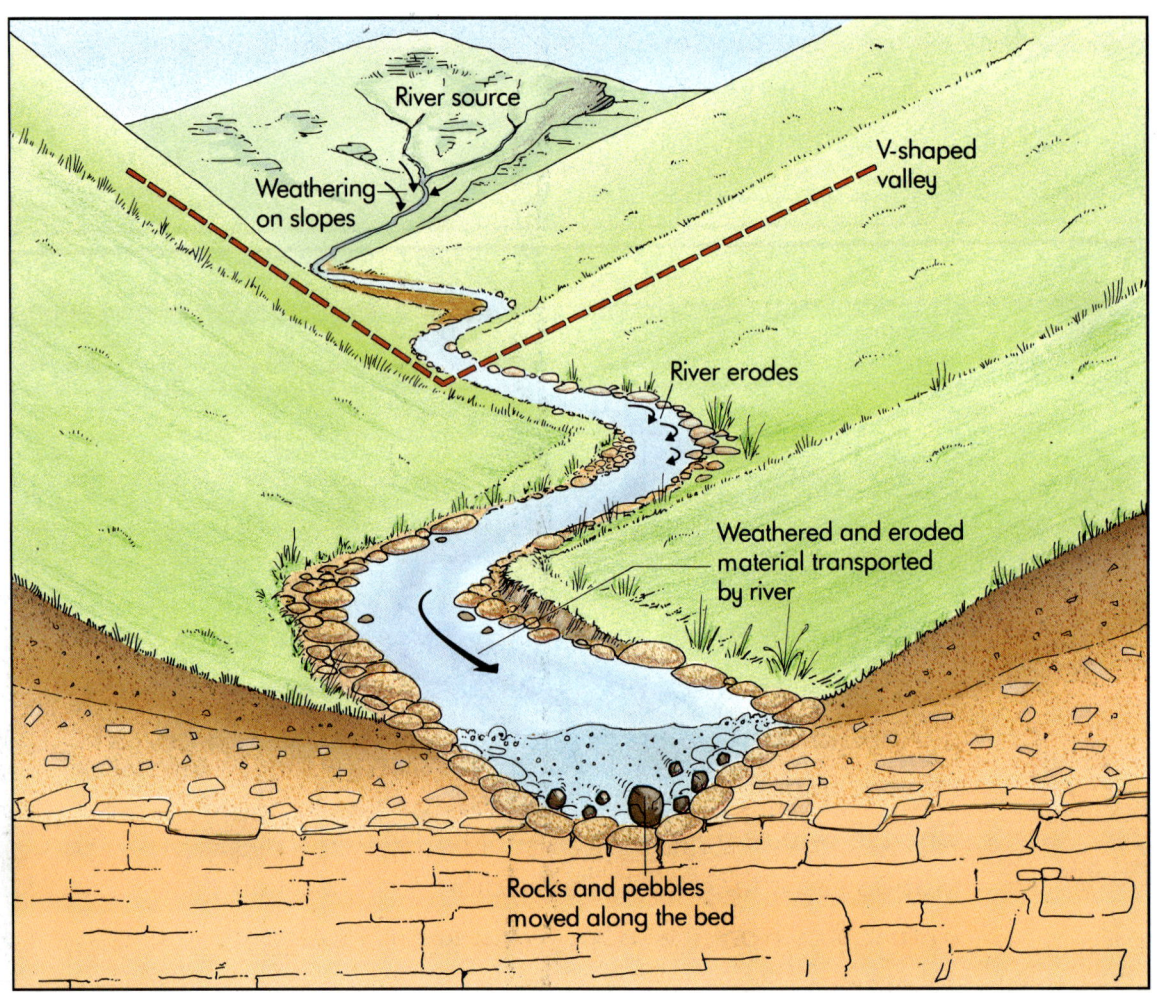

Picture A V-shaped valley

As the channel gets deeper, the steep sides become weaker and begin to break up. More loose soil and rock slides down into the channel and is carried away by the stream. The result is a small valley with steep sides. It is called a V-shaped valley. The pieces of rock also get damaged as they bounce along the channel bed. In the end they become smooth pebbles.

Looking at our Environment

Further away from the source, the river and channel become bigger. The river makes its way down from high land. It follows the easiest route down the valley, but it rarely goes straight. In the photo, the river is winding around the **spurs** in the valley.

A winding river Photo A

Things to do

1. Make a list of all the words about rivers that you have learned so far. Can you remember what they all mean?

2. Copy the following and use these words to fill in the blank spaces: erode boulders seaside
   The rock fragments in rivers help to ____ the channel bed. Very large rocks called ____ will sometimes fall into the channel from the valley sides. As they get bounced along they become rounded and smooth. Somewhere else that this happens is at the ____.

3. Look at Photo A. Describe the photo carefully using the words that you know about rivers.

13 How a river floods and feeds

As a river makes its way towards the sea, the channel and valley get much bigger. Streams (called **tributaries**) join the main river, bringing water from other places. The bends in a river also have a special name. They are called **meanders**. On the outside of the bend the water flows more quickly than the inside so there is more erosion. But on the inside of the bend, because the river is moving more slowly, bits of rock and soil drop out. This is called **deposition**.

Look carefully at the diagram of a 'slice' of a river.

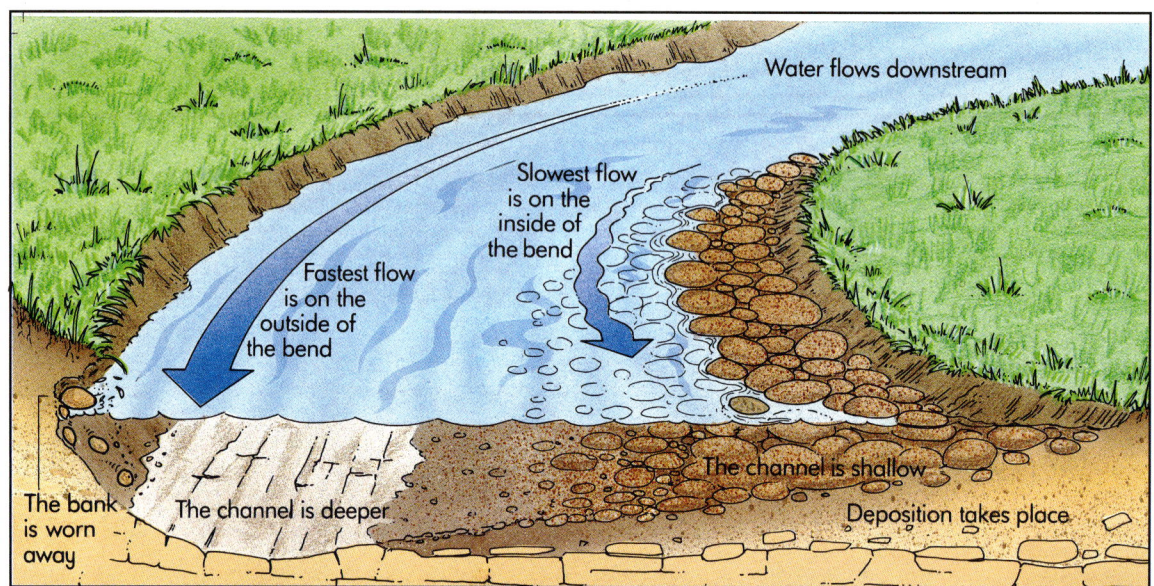

A slice of river

When a river gets to the flat land in a **lowland valley** it is wide and the meanders become very big.

Photo A River meanders

28

Looking at our Environment

At certain times of year the river may become too full and overflow. The water spills over the banks of the river channel onto the **flood plain**.

When this happens the river leaves behind a lot of stony earthy **sediment**, after the water has drained away. This helps to form a very good fertile soil for growing crops, though it may also cause damage to people's homes.

At last the river reaches the sea. By now it is very wide. Where it joins the sea is called the **river mouth**.

River mouth Photo B

Things to do

1. Use an atlas to find the following rivers in the British Isles: Severn, Thames, Trent. Mark them on Activity Sheet 16. Choose one river and also mark on its tributaries and mouth.
2. Find out which rivers are found near the following places: Liverpool, Belfast, Edinburgh, Newcastle. Mark them on too. What do you notice about the last place and the name of the river?
3. Use a map of the world and find the River Ganges and the River Nile. Name the countries where these rivers are found. What main settlements can you find near the mouth of these rivers?
4. Write a newspaper story to show what is good and what is bad about a river flooding.

14 World weather

Since many parts of the world have different weather from the British Isles, it isn't too surprising that the soils are different. This is partly because soils are affected by the amount of sun, rain and wind. The **natural vegetation** and the crops that are grown also vary.

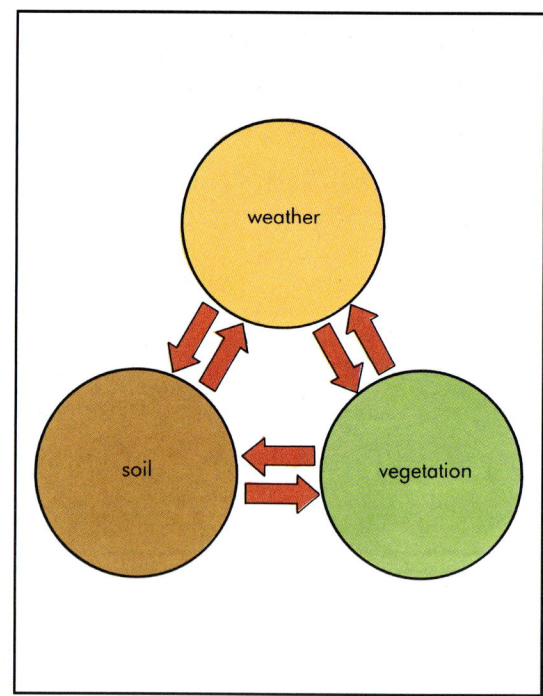

Picture A
How the weather affects the soil and what we can grow in it

Finding out about the physical environment is important to help us understand where and why people live in different parts of the world.

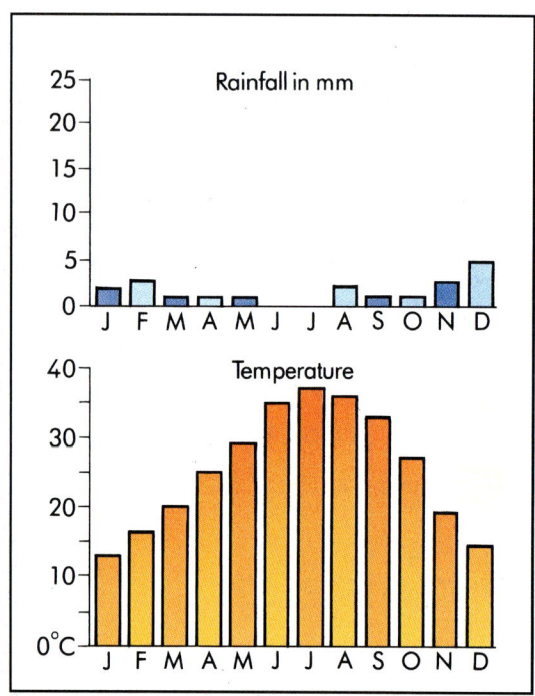

In the Sahara Desert in Africa, for example, the weather is very hot and dry in the daytime, but at night it is very cold. It hardly ever rains there and the soils are very dry, sandy and stony. They are not fertile and few plants are able to grow there. Those that do are specially adapted to live in poor soil without very much water.

Picture B
Rainfall and temperature in the Sahara desert

Looking at our Environment

Few plants are able to grow in the desert, so there is no leaf litter which would help to make the soil more fertile. Because of the harsh physical environment, few people live in the Sahara desert. The people who do live there cannot grow any crops because there is not enough rainfall in the year, so they move from place to place to find food and water for their families and animals. They are called **nomads**.

Photo A   Nomads in tent villages

Things to do

1. Use an atlas to find the Sahara desert. Find out more about the vegetation and climate for the whole of Africa from other maps in the atlas. Do the vegetation and climate patterns in these maps match up with the settlement patterns in Africa? Tracing the different maps may help you.
2. Find out about another part of the world where tropical rainforest forms the natural vegetation. Fill in the chart on Activity Sheet 18 to compare this place with the desert and the British Isles. You will need to find information on the following: weather, vegetations, soils and number of people. Use an atlas to help you.

15 Soil on the move

Soil is such an important resource to people. But if we don't look after it properly, it doesn't stay in the places where it is needed most.

Wind and water (rainfall and rivers) cause soil to erode naturally. However, when people disturb the natural vegetation of a place by farming, erosion is more likely to happen. This is because the roots have been cut that bound the soil together.

Hundreds of years ago, most of England's natural woodland vegetation was cleared to plant crops. The land was divided into fields. Stone walls and hedgerows were made, to protect the cleared areas from wind erosion.

Photo A Stone walls

In recent years many of these walls and hedges have been removed to make bigger fields which are easier to farm using modern machines. As a result, the soil has become badly eroded.

Photo B Modern farming

Looking at our Environment

In other regions of the world like the Himalayas, for example, heavy **monsoon** rains and melting snow on steep mountain slopes cause natural erosion. Luckily, there are forests which protect the soil on the steep slopes. People have made the erosion much worse by cutting down the trees for firewood, or to grow crops.

As a result, the soil has been washed away and the land has become less fertile. Meanwhile, the muddy rivers carrying away the eroded soil may ruin water supplies downstream. Wildlife may be affected and in lowland areas flooding may occur.

Photo C Erosion in the Himalayas

Things to do

1. Use an atlas to find out where the eroded soil from the Himalayas goes to. Use what you have learned about rivers to help you.
2. Look at Photo C. How does the forest help to keep the soil in place?
3. Many other materials can erode and in many different ways. Talk about these and see how many different ideas you can come up with.

16 Where's the nearest volcano?

Etna, Vesuvius, Mt St Helens, Fuji, Krakatoa are all famous **volcanoes** that you may have heard about on the news or in history books. These volcanoes have become 'famous' because of the hazard they have caused to people's lives, homes and land.

Photo A Non-active volcano

This map of the world shows all the different places where there are active volcanoes. You can see that a pattern forms. This is because the **Earth's crust** isn't quite as solid as you might think!

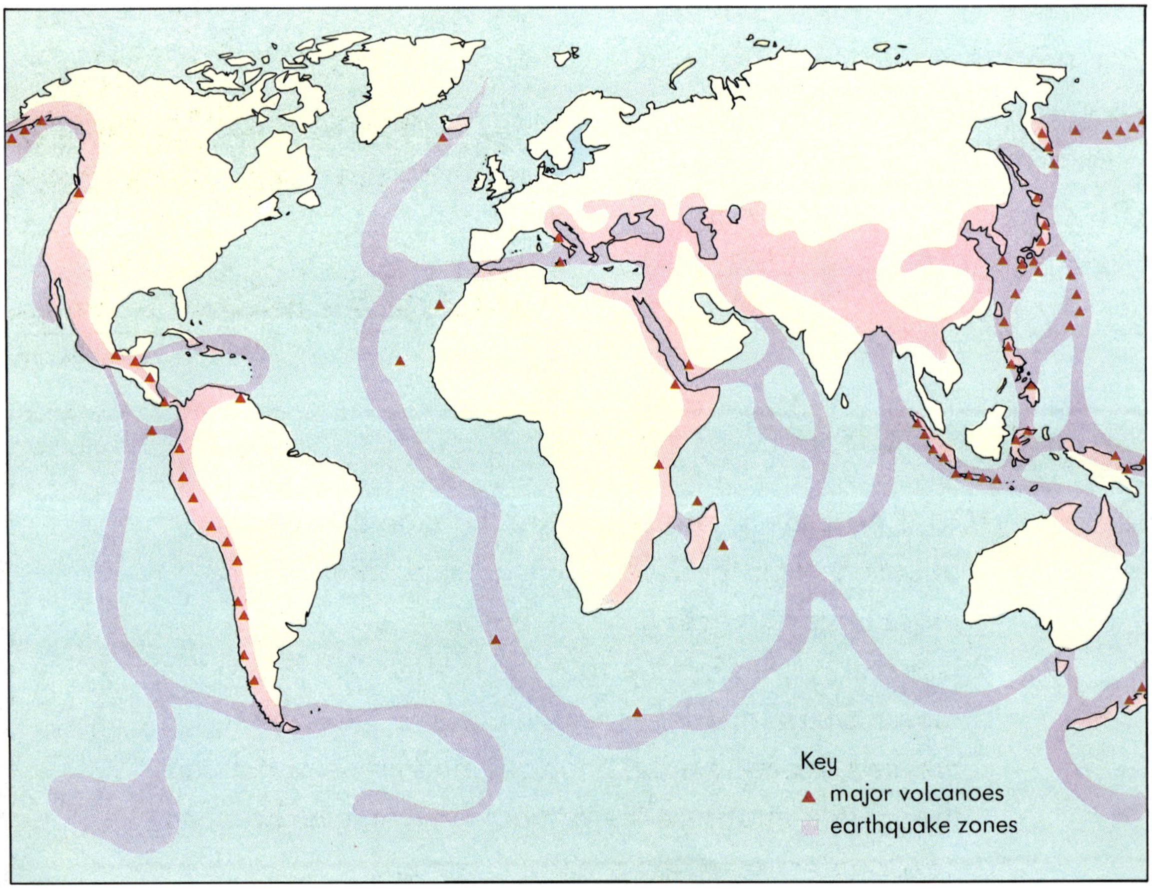

Key
▲ major volcanoes
▨ earthquake zones

Map A Places at risk from volcanoes

Looking at our Environment

Underneath all of the oceans, land and mountains, the earth's crust is made up of a number of huge sections called **plates**. The edges of these plates don't quite fit together and they don't stay still. The plates are so big that where they move, even only a little, different types of volcanic activity may happen.

Photo B An active volcano

Things to do

1. Find the five volcanoes named on page 34 on maps of Europe and the world. Do you think that there is a risk of volcanic activity in the British Isles?
2. Use the map of Europe on Activity Sheet 20. Two places where there is a risk of volcanic activity are marked. Name them. London is marked as well. Use the scale to measure the straight line distance between London and each of the places marked.

17 Volcanoes – not just hot-headed mountains!

Volcanic activity takes place at the edges of plates in the Earth's crust. Hot **lava** and **ash** are forced towards the earth's surface through cracks in the crust. Lava is molten rock; when it cools down it hardens. Each time a volcano erupts, another layer of lava pours out. These layers build up to form a **volcanic cone**.

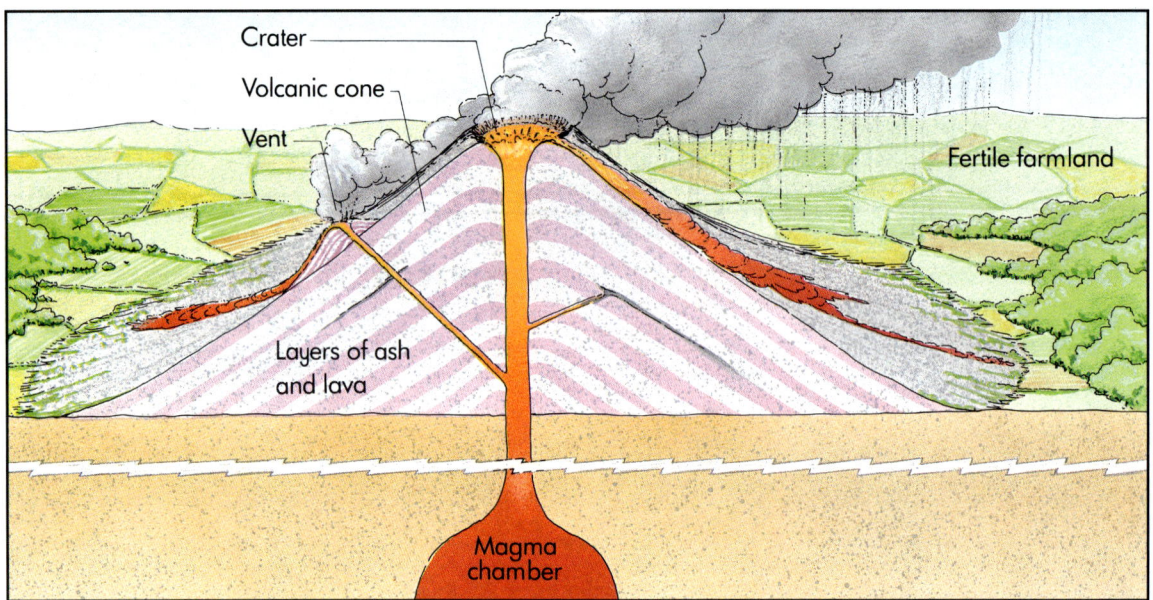

Picture A Volcanic mountain

Volcanoes are not always sudden, fiery and dangerous. In places, such as the Giant's Causeway in Ireland, the lava reached the surface much more slowly and did not form a volcanic mountain. When it cooled it formed rock called **basalt** (see Photo A).

Sometimes the molten lava does not reach the surface and it fills up some of the cracks in the crust. This eventually cools to form other rocks.

Photo A Giant's Causeway, Ireland

Looking at our Environment

In some volcanic areas, good fertile soils will form as the lava and ash material become eroded. So in spite of the hazards, many people still live near them. In Indonesia, for example, there are many areas of volcanic activity and a very high population density.

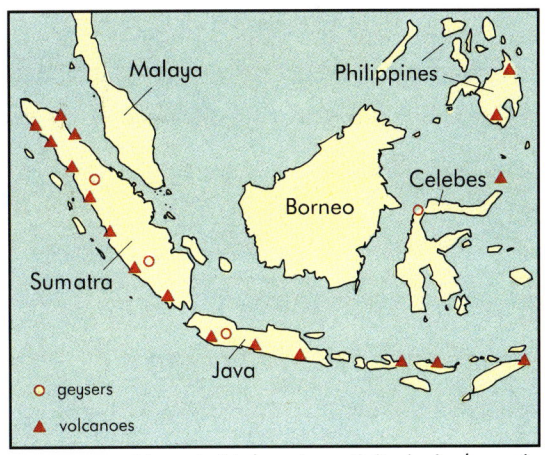

Map A Volcanic activity in Indonesia

Photo B Farming in Indonesia

Things to do

1. Draw your own diagram of a volcanic mountain. Add labels to show the main features.
2. Imagine that you live near a volcano. Write a story to say why you live there and what might make you decide to move away.

18 When the earth moves

Other major hazards are found in the same types of places as volcanoes. They are caused by the movement of the earth's crust at the edges of plates. The most famous are the **earthquakes** that you may have heard about in the news, but others include **tidal waves**, **landslides** and **avalanches**.

Earthquakes do not happen on a regular basis. Although scientists use special equipment to detect any movement underground, they cannot always predict exactly when or where an earthquake may occur. In China and Japan, scientists have also been studying how animals seem to know when an earthquake is about to happen.

Picture A 'An earthquake is coming'

I	Imperceptible	Detected only by instruments
II	Very weak	Detected by sensitive people at rest
III	Weak	Loose objects may be disturbed slightly
IV	Moderate	Rattling of doors and windows; some sleepers awake
V	Fairly strong	Most sleepers awake; noticed out of doors
VI	Strong	Furniture overthrown; cracking of plaster
VII	Very strong	Some damage to buildings
VIII	Destructive	Walls crack; chimneys fall
IX	Very destructive	Severe damage; some buildings destroyed
X	Devastating	Foundations, roads, pipes etc. damaged
XI	Catastrophic	Few buildings survive; fissures in ground
XII	Major catastrophe	Complete destruction; crumpling of ground

Picture B The Mercalli Scale

During an earthquake, a **seismograph** is used to measure the amount that the earth shakes or 'quakes'.

The effects of a large earthquake tend to be more serious in places where many people live. Buildings, homes, roads and railways may all be damaged. People are often killed because of falling buildings. The Mercalli scale is used to measure how much damage an earthquake causes. We can also use it to compare the strength of different earthquakes.

Looking at our Environment

After an earthquake a lot of help is needed to clear up and to make sure that the people have shelter, clean water and food.

In poorer areas of the world this is always a difficult task and richer countries usually try to help out by sending blankets, tents, food and medical supplies.

Photo A After an earthquake in Sicily

Things to do

1. Imagine that there has been a serious earthquake in a mountainous area of Turkey. It is the middle of winter and the area is very snowy. Most people have lost their homes. Your school is to be used as the United Kingdom base for all the supplies that must be sent out to help the people there.

    Draw a sketch plan of your school and grounds and use a key to show where all the important supplies will be collected, delivered and stored.

2. The local newspapers want to help you appeal for supplies and help, but they need to know some basic details about earthquakes to write their story. Write a letter to the editor of the paper to tell her the basic things you know about the hazard of earthquakes and how they happen.

19 A world full of resources?

 Within the different physical environments around the world, there are many natural resources which are very useful to people. The problem is that people often take these resources for granted and forget that they may be hard to replace.

Photo A Deforestation in the rainforest

Wood, coal, metal, food and water are some of the important resources that we use every day. If these are not taken carefully, the environment and the surrounding area may be badly disturbed or damaged.

As well as food and water, wood is one of the most useful basic resources all around the world. It can be used for fire, buildings, furniture and paper.

It is possible to plant trees and replace the ones that have been removed, but in some parts of the world, especially in the tropical rainforests, this does not often happen.

Looking at our Environment

Forests like these may now need special protection to slow down the rate that trees are being taken away. In some countries, special planning laws have been made to protect the environment, and to mend the damage that has been done. For example, in the pine forests of Scandinavia, large areas of trees are chopped down every year to produce timber for buildings and to make paper, but new trees are always planted to replace them.

Photo B Fir plantation

Things to do

1. Make a list of ten things in your bedroom that are made from natural resources. Compare your list with your classmates'.
2. Mark on the map on Activity Sheet 23 where these resources may have come from.

20 The ancient forests versus the beefburger

In many of the world's tropical rainforests, large areas have been cut down. These forests are chopped down not just for their good quality wood, but also so that the land can be used for grazing beef cattle. The forests' resources have not been replaced.

Picture A Does this hamburger cost the Earth?

Some people have benefited from this. They made money when the wood was sold for timber and the change to cattle grazing has provided new jobs.

But people who lived in the forest have lost their homes. Rare plants and animals have been destroyed and soil erosion has become very bad because of the heavy tropical rainfall on the bare earth.

It may be that by removing so much of the world's forests, people have caused a change in the climate.

Looking at our Environment

Photo A Life in the rainforest

Photo B Nowhere to hide

Things to do

1. Find out more about the tropical rainforests and the people who live there. Write an environmental fact sheet for your school, giving details of the benefits and problems of the removal of the rainforests.
2. Do a survey of other children in the school to find out whether they are for or against the rainforest clearance. Draw up a bar chart to show the results.

21 Looking after our environment

Not all environmental problems are big ones; small problems matter as well. Any area is at risk of damage if it is not well looked after.

All human activity changes the 'natural' landscape in some way, whether it is a settlement, road, railway, industrial factory, quarry, mine or rubbish dump.

Sometimes it is the job of the town or county council to look after and improve the local environment. Special groups have been set up to look after places that need special protection. There are laws to protect National Parks and places of historical and scientific interest.

Photo A National Park

Photo B Recycling cans

It is up to each person to help as well. This could mean anything from helping to clear out the local pond or picking up litter around the school, to organizing the collection of bottles for recycling.

Looking at our Environment

Sometimes the big industrial companies that caused a problem make sure that the place is restored afterwards.

In cases like gravel extraction, people may accept the need to disturb the environment because jobs are created while the gravel is being **quarried**. The companies plan ahead to make sure that the area is restored or improved when quarrying stops. They may try to recreate the landscape as it was or they may create a new feature, like a lake.

Photo C Gravel works

Photo D Reclaimed gravel pit

Things to do

1. On Activity Sheet 24 describe an activity that you took part in at school to improve the environment there, or suggest one that your school could start.
2. Choose a place in your local area which you think could be restored or improved. Find out whether the local authority are planning to improve the place. What are their plans?

    If they have no plans, suggest some reasons why they haven't. How could you persuade them to change their minds?

Glossary

ash
The rocky and gritty substance ejected by a volcano.

aspect
The direction a place faces.

avalanche
A large mass of snow, rock or ice descending a mountain rapidly.

basalt
A dark, dense rock produced by volcanic activity.

channel
The bed where a natural stream of water runs. The bed of a river is the rock on the bottom.

densely/sparsely populated
Area where lots of/few people live.

deposition
The act or process of depositing (letting fall as sediment).

Earth's crust
The outer rocky portion of the Earth.

earthquake
Shaking of Earth's surface due to faults in the crust.

employment
The jobs that people do.

erosion
The gradual wearing away of the earth's surface by water (river, waves, rainfall), wind or glacial ice.

flood plain
Level land that may be submerged by floodwaters.

landscape
Features which give the land its shape, for example, mountains, beaches, valleys.

landslide
The rapid downward movement of a mass of rock or earth on a mountain or cliff.

lava
Fluid rock that flows from a volcano. When it cools down it hardens into rock.

lowland valley
Low or level area of land drained by a river and its tributaries.

magma chamber
An area of semi-fluid material lying beneath the Earth's crust.

Looking at our Environment

meander
A turn or winding of a river.

mental map
A picture in your head of an area that you know or of a route you often take.

monsoon
A south west wind in South Asia, especially in the Indian Ocean, which brings heavy rain.

natural resource
A resource that occurs naturally in the environment, for example, wood, soil, water.

natural vegetation
Plants, such as trees, grass, which grow without having been planted by humans.

nomads
People who wander in search of pasture and water for their families and animals.

Ordnance Survey map
A detailed map of an area, drawn to scale, using symbols which are explained in a key, to represent features.

parent material
The rocky layer underneath soil. It is called parent material as over time it breaks down to form soil.

permeable/impermeable
Does/doesn't permit fluids to pass through it.

plate
Rigid section of the Earth's crust.

population
The total number of people living in a settlement, region or country.

quarry
To obtain rock by cutting or blasting. The place where the rock is obtained from is also called a quarry.

rill
A very small stream.

river basin
The area drained by a river and its tributaries.

river mouth
Where a river reaches the sea (or lake).

scale
A line on a map indicating the length used to show a large unit of measure, for example, 1 cm on the map might be equal to 1 km.

sediment
Material deposited by water, wind or glaciers.

seismograph
Instrument showing force or direction of an earthquake.

settlement
A group of buildings which can be homes or a mixture of homes, shops, offices etc.

soil
The upper layer of earth in which plants grow. Top soil contains dead leaves, twigs and worms which help to make it fertile. Sub-soil is the soil lying immediately under the top soil. It is not as good and there are more stones.

source (of a river)
Place where a river starts.

spur
A ridge that breaks through the sloping sides of a valley.

symbols
Signs used to represent features on a map without drawing a picture of them.

tidal wave
An unusually high large ocean wave, that sometimes follows an earthquake.

tributaries
A stream or river which flows into another.

volcanic cone
Conical mountain formed by layers of lava building up.

volcano
An opening in the earth's crust from which molten or hot lava, ash and steam erupt.

waterlogged
When a permeable surface has so much water on it no more can soak in.